South Carolina Ghosts

SWEETWATER
    PRESS

South Carolina Ghosts
Copyright © 2006 by Sweetwater Press
Produced by Cliff Road Books

ISBN-13: 978-1-58173-565-9
ISBN-10: 1-58173-565-0

Book design by Pat Covert
Cover photo courtesy of National Oceanic and
Atmospheric Administration/Department of Commerce

Printed in the United States of America

South Carolina Ghosts

they are among us

Lynne L. Hall

SWEETWATER
PRESS

Table of Contents

They Are Among Us

They Are Among Us

I won't lie to you. I'm a skeptic. I mean, like everyone else, I grew up shivering delightedly to ghost stories. But for the most part, I believed my mama when she told me, "There're no such things as ghosts."

Later on, I spent a lot of time examining the world around me and trying to fit it all into one mold or the other. Religion? Or science? The great debate. One entirely spiritual, based on faith. The other, entirely logical, based on scientific evidence.

For many years, I fell solidly on the science side. It was that evidence thing that got me. So, I spent a lot of time and effort ignoring the things that didn't fit my mold, chalking them up to coincidence or serendipity.

But years bring wisdom, and, if you're lucky, they open your heart and mind. I was lucky. I had an experience with the spiritual realm, a realm we can't see or touch, but one we know in our hearts exists.

It happened days after the death of Oleta—a woman who was dear to me, a woman who'd parented me as much, if not more, than my own parents. In the

8

performance of my duties as a professional firefighter, I was about to go into a burning house. At the moment I crawled over the threshold, I heard Oleta's voice in my head: "Be careful, Lynne." In that moment I knew she was there, watching over me.

That experience brought a realization that, yes, there's scientific evidence for some things. But there're many other things that simply can't be explained by science, things that can only be known in your own heart. I found there was a place for both realms—that the spiritual could exist side by side with the logical.

Still, when it came to actual ghosts, I remained skeptical. So, I approached this project with a sense of fun, searching out stories that would be fun to tell and entertaining to read.

I found them, but I also found something else. I found stories with a common thread. In each story, there is a strong connection between the spirits and the places they were haunting. And there was something in their lives that, in death, seems to keep them bound to this world. Perhaps the death was a violent or sudden one. Or perhaps there was a loss of a great love. Whatever the reason, they're here. And they've made themselves known. They've been

9

seen. They've been heard. And they can't be explained away by science.

It's enough to make a skeptic wonder if, indeed, they are among us.

Lynne L. Hall

Tales of a Haunted City

Tales of a Haunted City

Nowhere in America will you find a city richer in history than Charleston, South Carolina. First called Charles Towne in honor of England's King Charles II, Charleston was the first permanent settlement in South Carolina. It was established in 1670 by a group of two hundred colonists from Barbados.

The early days were, no doubt, wild and woolly, with the town often subject to attack from Spain and France, who still laid claim to the land, as well as from Native American pirates. Despite this, Charleston's lucrative sea faring trade and its religious tolerance made it a popular site for settlers. By 1742, it was the fourth largest city in America, with a hugely diverse population that blended English, French, Scottish, German, and Iberian cultures.

Charleston played a pivotal role throughout American history. Two signers of the Declaration of Independence were born here, and three were jailed for treason in Charleston's Provost Dungeon. Its rich

Carolina soil, perfect for the cultivation of rice and indigo, spawned a rise in gentlemen planters and, combined with its shipping industry and unfortunately, its slave trade, the city soon became the cultural and economic center of the South. In addition, the first shot of the Civil War occurred here, when Confederate soldiers fired on Fort Sumter.

Thanks to the fact that General William Sherman was once posted here and seemed to have a soft spot in his heart for the city, Charleston was spared the razing experienced by most Southern cities. And where Sherman left off in preserving the city, Charleston's good citizens picked up. Acutely aware of their place in American history, they have diligently worked for decades to preserve and restore Charleston's numerous historic homes and buildings. Centered in Charleston's historic district, these buildings number more than one thousand four hundred and include the three hundred-year-old homes of rice lords and shipping magnates, antebellum homes, historic civic buildings, churches, and even cemeteries.

You know what this means don't you? I bet you do. I bet you know that all these historic buildings, filled with so much history, mean a plethora of ghost stories.

13

From patriots to pirates, from gentried gentleman to ladies of the evening, from frightened slaves to headless torsos, Charleston has certainly earned its reputation as "America's Most Haunted City."

The Old Exchange Building and Provost Dungeon

Because of its extensive shipping trade, its rice and indigo exports, and its unfortunate slave trade, Charles Towne developed into the fourth largest city and was one of the wealthiest towns in colonial America. This phenomenal growth in trade necessitated the construction of a building to accommodate the heavy import-export market and to provide a place to conduct both public and private business.

Charles Towne's first effort in urban planning, the Exchange and Custom House was designed to reflect the self-image of the town's elite. The town fathers chose the foot of Broad Street as the site for their new building. The center of the waterfront, it was an area where inland streams converged with major maritime traffic thoroughfares, and had long been the symbolic center of the city.

Several important civic buildings had once

occupied the site, including the Half-Moon Battery, an original fortification of Charles Towne. In the name of urban planning, adjacent street markets were moved to another block because they were unsightly.

The Exchange Building was erected in 1771. Shiploads of cut, dressed, and beveled Portland stone were imported for the building's façade. It was one of the most important buildings in Charles Towne—indeed in the whole of colonial America. The last building built by the British government in the American colonies, it served as the office for the king's customs collector and was used as a space for public gatherings and lavish entertainment.

It was elegantly constructed in the popular Palladian architecture style, but its design and the construction materials were unique for the time. Only two other colonial buildings—Philadelphia's Town Hall and Boston's Faneuil Hall—came close in stature, but even those venerable buildings could not match the architectural distinction of Charles Towne's new Exchange and Custom House.

Perhaps the town fathers didn't exactly have that urban planning thing down pat, though, for they decided to use the nether regions of their fine and elegant Exchange Building as a dungeon. Called the Provost Dungeon, it was a damp, unwholesome cellar located deep beneath the Exchange Building. Men and women prisoners, transported in irons, were crowded together in squalor.

Despite the fact that the Exchange and Custom House was built and, for a time, was controlled by the British, it played an important role in American history. In 1773, Charles Towne citizens met in the building's Great Hall to protest the Tea Act. While the citizens of Boston dumped their tea into the harbor, in Charles Towne tea was seized and stored in the Exchange Building and was later sold to fund the patriot cause.

In 1774, South Carolina's delegates to the Continental Congress, the group that drafted the Declaration of Independence, were elected in the Great Hall. Then, in 1776, South Carolina declared independence on the steps of the Exchange Building and Custom House. Charles Towne was the birthplace of two signers of the Declaration of Independence, Arthur Middleton and Edward Rutledge. After they penned their names to that venerable document, they, along with St. Luke's Parish native Thomas Heywood Jr., found themselves charged with treason by the

British and tossed for a while into the filthy dungeon.

They weren't the only patriots jailed. In 1780, after a lengthy siege, the British marched into Charles Towne and took over. They jailed leading citizens in the dungeon, requiring that they sign an oath to the King to secure their release.

Isaac Hayne was a South Carolina patriot who took the oath of allegiance to avoid imprisonment. His entire family was ill with small pox in Charles Towne, and being incarcerated was not an option at that time. He was assured by the British that he would not be required to take up arms against his country. The British, however, broke their promise and drafted him into the Royal army.

They broke theirs, so he could break his, Hayne reasoned. He rejoined the American Army and fought against the British, who unfortunately captured him. He was thrown into the Provost Dungeon and was charged with treason. Without a jury trial, he was convicted and hanged within forty-eight hours. His execution was controversial and caused the two British officers who sentenced him and carried out the execution many problems for years to come.

As Hayne was being paraded through Charles

Towne on the way to the gallows, his sister reportedly called out to him, "Come back, Isaac! Come back!" To which her brother replied, "I will if I can."

Many believe that Isaac Hayne has kept his promise. It's his ghost, they say, that haunts the Provost Dungeon and the Old Exchange Building, which now operates as a museum. Ghost tours also are conducted here, and reportedly on several occasions, there have been strange occurrences—unexplained shadows on the walls, chains swinging or rattling, strange noises—that were so frightening, entire tour groups broke and ran from the dungeon.

In addition to the ghost of Isaac Hayne, many believe the ghosts of Charleston's many pirates haunt the Old Exchange Building. In the late 1700s, Charles Towne was a favorite port for some of the Atlantic's most notorious pirates. The infamous Blackbeard, as a matter of fact, held the entire city for ransom, capturing vessels sailing into the harbor and taking hostages at will. He refused to release the hostages unless the town gave him much needed medical supplies.

Although many think the Old Exchange Building could be haunted by ol' Blackbeard himself, it makes more sense that the ghost is another famous pirate. See, Blackbeard met his fate elsewhere, but Stede Bonnet, known as the "Gentleman Pirate," was captured, along with his crew, in December 1718. Bonnet and twenty-two of his crew were hanged on December 10, 1718, at White Point. It seems likely that it's these old buccaneers who may be responsible for much of the building's poltergeist activity, which includes unexplained images and the balls of light known as "orbs" seen in many photographs taken here. Orbs and other flashes of light often captured on film are thought to be ghostly presences that are either too shy or too weak to make an appearance.

Dock Street Theater

The original Dock Street Theater was the first theater to be built in America. It opened on February 12, 1736, with a bawdy Restoration farce by George Farhquar entitled *The Recruiting Officer*. The theater was located on the corner of Dock and Church Streets, facing Dock Street, which was later renamed Queen Street.

For the next several years, the theater featured plays and operas and was a popular Charleston attraction. Its true fate is unknown, but it's presumed that it was burned in 1740, when a huge fire devoured the city's historic French section.

In 1809, a hotel was built on the site by Alexander Calder and his wife. The couple renovated several buildings on the Church Street side, adding a grand stairway and a drawing room. The Planter's Hotel offered superior lodging, excellent food, and innovative drinks—it's the home of the Planter's Punch, a tasty and fruity little rum concoction. It became popular with planters from middle South Carolina, who came to town for some fun and relaxation during the horseracing season.

In 1835, the hotel was remodeled, with the addition of a wrought iron balcony, whose silhouette against the spire of St. Philip's Episcopal Church has become one of the most photographed images in the city. For fifty years, the hotel was the principal hotel in Charleston, popular with plantation owners and seafaring merchants alike.

During these heyday years, the Planter's Hotel became the home of Nettie Dickerson. Nettie moved to Charleston in 1838 and took a job at St. Philip's church, located across the street from the hotel. Nettie was a comely miss, but at age twenty-five, she was considered past her marrying prime.

What's a girl to do? Initially, Nettie decided if she couldn't get a man of her own, she'd take someone else's. Her job at the church gave her the opportunity to meet many church members looking for a little action on the side, and she became mistress to a succession of men, none of whom was willing to leave his family for her.

Eventually, she began to resent their hypocrisy in sitting piously on the front pew at church every Sunday, after spending Saturday night drinking and carousing with her. On one stormy evening, as she was about to enter the church, a lightning bolt crackled overhead. It jagged its way across the sky and struck the cross on the church spire. Hmm, thought Nettie, must be a sign from God.

I'm thinking she misinterpreted that sign, however. The next day, she quit her job at the church, vowing that she'd have more out of life. She then moved into the Planter's Hotel and began a new career—in the world's oldest profession. Nettie was good at her job and she soon became a wealthy woman, though she was, of course, snubbed by the "polite" society of Charleston.

Through her years at the Planter's Hotel, Nettie gained a reputation for her outrageous behavior. During violent rainstorms, she would don a bright red ball gown, and, having developed an affinity for lightning since her "epiphany," she would stand out on the hotel balcony watching the lightning crackle across the Charleston sky. On one such meteorologically active evening, God must've decided it was time to set her straight about her interpretation of his previous "sign." A lightning bolt streaked across the sky and struck the balcony railing where Nettie had rested her hands. She was immediately electrocuted.

One of the hotel's most famous guests during the time Nettie lived there was an actor named Junius Booth. An imposing entertainer with a full, rich, baritone, Booth stayed at the hotel when performing in Charleston. Booth was the father of three sons, two of whom also became actors. His most famous son did not earn his fame on stage, however. No, John Wilkes Booth's infamy came from the shot he made from a theater balcony—a shot that struck and killed President Abraham Lincoln.

After the Civil War, the Planter's Hotel went out of business and fell to disrepair. It was certain to simply disintegrate there on its foundation, but in 1930, the building became a Works Progress Administration project. It was restored, renovated, and reopened. It was taken over by the city of Charleston and was once again named the Dock Street Theater, even though Dock Street had long since been named Queen Street. Today the Dock Street Theater is home to the Charleston Stage Company, a community performing group. It also houses Charleston's Cultural Affairs office and The City Gallery, an exhibition venue for local artists.

It also, of course, is home to a couple of haunting spirits. Nettie Dickerson is one. She appears, most often wearing a gaudy red ball gown, on the theater's second floor. She floats around the theater, apparently unaware of anything going on around her. She never interacts with the living and may be totally oblivious to the fact that she's dead. Those who have seen her say one of the most frightening aspects about Nettie is that she seems to be walking—or floating, as the case may be—cut off at the knees. Seems when the theater was last restored, the second floor floorboards were raised twelve inches, which brings them to about Nettie's knees.

23

The other ghost that treads the floorboards of the Dock Street Theater is Junius Booth. No one is sure why he's chosen this particular theater, considering that he was a famous and well-traveled actor, but he has been seen enough times to earn his spot in the local ghost tours.

The Old City Jail

Night had fallen and rain had been pelting down on him for more than two hours, when ol' Jack the fur trader came upon the Six Mile House. The lights glowing from the inn's windows looked warm and inviting. "Finally," he thought, "a dry place to sleep."

"Come in, good sir! Come in." The inn's proprietess met him at the door. "Take off that wet cloak and sit by the fire. Ooooh, you are a big, strong fella, aren't you!" She cooed as he shed his wet outer garments.

Jack looked askance at the lady, a comely lass. Her flirty words, he thought, seemed inappropriate. "Thank ye, ma'am. It is a mite cold and wet out there. I'd appreciate a place to sleep tonight."

"Of course, of course. My name is Lavinia. And, what, handsome sir, is your name?"

"Jack," he replied. He was surprised as the lady

24

took his arm and led him over to a chair in front of the fire. Her manner was much too friendly for his taste. Jack had no illusions about his appeal to women. He basically had none. He was a big fella, true enough. But he was nothing to look at, with a pock-marked face and a nose that covered half his face. The straggly beard didn't help anything either. So he couldn't help but wonder why this beautiful woman was showing such an interest.

He'd heard about places where unsuspecting men would rent a bed for the night and never be seen again, murdered for their meager savings and belongings. He had no intention of letting it happen to him. He turned down the lady's offer of dinner, despite the fact that his stomach was rumbling at the savory aromas coming from the kitchen. He had strong suspicions that there might just be something a little extra in the food—like rat poison.

Miss Lavinia seemed disappointed at his refusal of her food. She pouted a bit, but eventually showed Jack to his room. Still suspicious, he made himself a pallet of his furs in one corner of the room, and placed other furs underneath the covers on the bed to make it look like he was slumbering peacefully beneath them. Then he crawled into his makeshift bed and eventually drifted off to sleep.

Late into the night, Jack was awakened by a sound. His heart pounded as he strained his ears, listening for the sound that had awakened him. Suddenly, there was a loud crash and when he looked across the room, there was an empty hole where the bed had been. It had dropped into the basement through a trap door. He crept over and looked down into the hole. There he saw John Fisher, Lavinia's husband, butcher knife in hand, furiously stabbing into the furs on the bed.

Scrambling, Jack grabbed his hat and cloak and dashed out into the rain. He didn't stop until he'd found the sheriff's office and reported his story of near murder. He even followed the sheriff's deputies back out to the inn, where a search of the basement beneath the trap door turned up a graveyard of skeletons.

Seems John and Lavinia Fisher had been at their murder game for quite some time. They would lull their guests into a warm, cozy sleep. Then, in the middle of the night, the guests' beds would drop into the basement and they would be stabbed to death. All their valuables would be added to the Fishers' assets.

John and Lavinia were tried, found guilty of murder,

and tossed into the Charleston City Jail to await execution. They were executed on the same day in 1820. John was first. "Please don't kill me," he pleaded. "It wasn't me. It was my wife. She made me do it!"

The rowdy crowd was unsympathetic. "Be a man!" They screamed.

After John was hanged, Lavinia was brought out. Dressed in her white wedding dress, she ascended the gallows stairs with an evil smile on her face. After stealing a quick kiss from her dead husband's lips, she turned to the crowd and in an unwavering voice screamed, "Do any of you have a message for the devil? I'll be glad to tell him!"

The crowd was silenced by her maniacal laughter as the rope was placed over her head. The snapping of her neck was the only sound heard when the lever was pulled and the floor dropped from under her. Lavinia Fisher was the first woman to be executed in the United States.

I guess the devil's still waiting for those messages from Lavinia, for, according to legend, she has yet to leave this earth. Seems her spirit is still hanging (sorry 'bout that) around the Old City Jail. And she may not be the only one.

27

Charleston's Old City Jail was constructed in 1802 and served as the city's jail until 1939. When first built, it consisted of four stories topped by a two-story octagonal tower. It was remodeled by Charleston architects Barbot and Seyle in 1855, at which time they added a rear octagonal wing, expansions to the main building, and Romanesque revival architectural details. The octagonal tower and the top story of the building were substantially damaged in the great earthquake of 1886, and those two elements were removed.

In addition to John and Lavina Fisher, Charleston's City Jail housed a variety of prisoners. The last of the nineteenth-century pirates were jailed here in 1822, as were the participants of the Denmark Vesey slave revolt. Denmark Vesey was a slave who, after winning a $1,500 lottery, purchased his freedom. He became prosperous and won respect from slaves and owners alike. His hatred of slavery drove him to organize a revolt to free all slaves. But he was betrayed, and he and other participants were held in the Old City Jail before their executions. In addition, during the Civil War, both Confederate and Union prisoners where held here.

The evil face of Lavinia Fisher is often glimpsed from a top story window, where she was held in a meager cell. By all accounts, she's a hostile ghost, especially to female visitors. She's also pretty strong, with the ability to fling objects across a room. She's been seen wandering the hallways of the jail—still wearing her white wedding dress. Reportedly, numerous psychics have tried to banish her spirit, but she refuses to leave.

Other spirits still haunting the jail include several members of the Denmark Vesey slave revolt and a Confederate soldier.

The Old Slave Market

In the eighteenth century, Charleston was the major point of entry for slaves being imported into the country. During this time, three out of four imported slaves were brought into Charleston and traded here. By 1790, city blacks outnumbered whites in Charleston, and curfew laws for slaves were enacted. At 10:00 p.m., bells would toll, and any slaves caught in the streets without written permission from their owners were jailed and severely beaten.

In 1808, foreign slave trade was abolished, but the

country's plantation economy depended heavily on slave labor. This led to the creation of a domestic slave trading system, and Charleston again became the major center for slave collecting and selling.

Plantation owners traveled from all over the country to buy and sell their slaves in Charleston, helping to make the city into the cultural and commercial hub of early America. During the antebellum period, Charleston also was the center of commercial activity for the South's plantation economy.

For many years, the slave trade was carried out in the street on the right side of the Exchange and Custom House. But in 1856, a city ordinance was passed that prohibited trading in the streets. No problem. The slave traders simply built a series of buildings with sales rooms on Chalmers, Queen, and State streets.

The largest of these slave markets was owned by Thomas Ryan, a sheriff and Charleston city alderman. Occupying the land between Chalmers and Queen streets, Ryan's Mart—now the Old Slave Mart—contained a shed with an arched entranceway, where slaves were traded; a four-story brick building, with offices and a jail, where slaves were held before trade; a kitchen; and a morgue.

When slaves were traded in the shed, they were displayed on auction tables, three feet high and ten feet long. According to legend, fiddlers were employed at the slave markets, a carryover from the foreign import days. In those days, the fiddlers played music for the slaves to dance to but not for the entertainment of the slaves or the customers. The dancing was intended to loosen the muscles of the slaves, which might have become atrophied during their long voyage from Africa—to make them more marketable.

The last slave auction was held in Ryan's Slave Market in 1863. Around 1878, the Slave Mart was renovated and used as a two-story tenement. It changed hands many times in the next few years, and was even used for a time as an auto repair shop. In 1938, it was bought by Charleston resident Miriam Wilson, who turned it into a museum featuring African and African-American arts and crafts. It was placed on the National Register of Historic Places in 1973. The museum was closed in 1987, but, recognizing the historical significance of the Old Slave Mart, the city of Charleston purchased the property in 1988.

Today, the Old Slave Mart, located on one of Charleston's only remaining cobblestone streets, is once again being operated as a museum. It's the only remaining building once used for slave trading in South Carolina. The museum, with its story of African-American history and the city's slave trade, is just one effort Charleston is making to face its ignoble history in the trade of human flesh.

As for the haunted history of the Old Slave Mart, there have been numerous reports of the echoing sounds of dancing feet as well as sightings of slaves in chains.

Charleston City Hall

In 1801, Charleston's city fathers constructed an elegant building to serve as a branch of the First Bank of the United States. One of eight branches, Charleston's branch served as the Office of Discount and Deposit.

The building's design is attributed to Charleston gentleman architect Gabriel Manigault. The building is constructed in the Adamesque architecture style, also known as Federal. This style, popular in Europe during the 1800s, interprets the Neoclassical style and uses decorative motifs of Roman art, such as sphinxes, scrolls, medallions, and urns.

The building's semi-circular projection on the north side and its round basement windows are characteristic of a Manigault design. The original red brick, trimmed in striking white Italian marble, was covered in stucco in 1882. Inside, a bulge was placed in the iron railing of the second floor balcony to accommodate the ladies' wide hoop skirts.

Congress revoked the bank's charter in 1811, and the building was turned over to the city of Charleston. It became the City Hall in 1818, and city council meetings have been held there ever since, making it the second oldest council chamber in the country. When the mayor and council meet here twice a month, they sit at the original Charleston-made 1818 black walnut desks.

Throughout the years, the city has acquired many paintings and objets d'art, each with a special connection to Charleston, which are displayed within City Hall. Among the paintings are two portraits of General Pierre G.T. Beauregard, the Confederate general in charge of the first battle of the Civil War.

Beauregard was an officer in the United States Army when the Civil War began. He immediately offered his services to the Confederacy and was placed in command of the defenses of Charleston. When Union Major Robert Anderson refused to evacuate Fort Sumter, it was Beauregard who led the attack on the fort. The April 12, 1861, shelling of Fort Sumter with canon fire is considered the first battle of the Civil War. When Anderson finally evacuated—with no lives lost on either side—Beauregard emerged a hero.

In his next engagement, he and General Joseph Johnston led Confederate troops to victory in the first Battle of Bull Run. He moved on to Tennessee, where he took over command of the Battle of Shiloh when General A.S. Johnston was killed. He almost won it, too, but he called off the attack prematurely on the second day. When General Ulyssess Grant's forces were reinforced, Beauregard found it necessary to retreat.

Beauregard was sent back to defend Charleston from September 1862 until April 1864, a chore he masterfully carried out. As a cultural and commercial hub, Charleston was considered an important target for the Union. During his time in the city, Beauregard successfully defended against formidable siege operations commanded by Union General Gillmore and Admirals Dupont and Dahlgren.

In May 1864, Beauregard re-enforced General

34

Robert E. Lee in the defense of Richmond, Virginia, defeating General Benjamin Butler in the Bermuda Hundred Campaign near Drewry's Bluff in his most brilliant battle to date. Following this resounding success against Bulter, Beauregard began believing his own press. Developing delusions of grandeur, he proposed to Lee and Confederate President Jefferson Davis that he lead a grand invasion of the North. He'd defeat Butler first, see. Next he'd hit Grant and his forces. With his superior military skills, it'd be no problem to take 'em out in short order. And, voilà! The North would be his…uh…theirs!

Lee and Davis weren't convinced. To get Beauregard out of their hair, Davis sent him to command the forces in the west. Since all of his forces were engaged elsewhere, Beauregard was unable to stop General William Sherman's forces in their March to the Sea. He surrendered, along with his old buddy J.E. Johnston, in April 1865.

After the war, Beauregard returned to Louisiana, where he wrote several books on the Civil War and engaged in a war of words with Davis. The two published bitter attacks on each other, each blaming the other for the defeat of the Confederacy.

He also served in the government and became involved with the railroads. He served as president of New Orleans, Jackson, & Mississippi Railroad and president of the New Orleans & Carrollton Street Railway, for which he invented a system of cable-powered street railway cars.

Beauregard is remembered fondly for his service in Charleston. Two portraits of the distinguished general hang in places of honor in the Charleston City Hall. The first was commissioned in New Orleans just as the Civil War was breaking out. Internationally-known artist George Healy began the portrait in New Orleans and, along with his brother Thomas, also an artist, followed Beauregard to Charleston to finish it. When Beauregard attacked Fort Sumter, the brothers left Charleston.

George, being a Northern man with Northern sympathies, returned to his home state of Massachusetts. Thomas, however, considered himself a Southern man, and returned to New Orleans. Because of his victory at Fort Sumter, another, smaller, portrait of Beauregard was commissioned—this time with Thomas doing the honors. He faithfully copied his brother's painting, but added two soldiers and a cannon in the lower left corner.

Perhaps it's the presence of these two portraits that have prompted Beauregard's return to Charleston. Maybe, an egoist even in death, he wants to live out eternity in a place where he was much admired. Whatever the reason, reports are that the spirit of Pierre Gustave Toutant Beauregard still wanders the halls of City Hall.

The 1843 Battery Carriage House Inn

The 1843 Battery Carriage House Inn

In addition to all of Charleston's well-known municipal buildings that are haunted, the 1843 Battery Carriage House Inn is a privately owned business with a ghost or two of its own.

The 1843 Battery Carriage House Inn was built as a home for Samuel Stevens in 1843, during Charleston's wealthiest days. In 1859, John F. Blalock, another wealthy Charlestonian, moved there, and was living there when the Civil War broke out. The area known as the Battery was bombarded extensively during the war and most houses, including the Blaylock house, sustained substantial damage.

After the war, Charleston entrepreneur Andrew Simonds, who had secreted money away in Liverpool before the war, founded the First National Bank of Charleston as well as the Imperial Fertilizer Company. He took over the Blaylock house in 1870 and commissioned John Henry Devereux, one of Charleston's most famous post-bellum architects, to design renovations that included the addition of a ballroom, library, and mansard roof.

Simonds used his home extensively for business and political entertainment. His family lived there for forty-five years. It was the childhood home of Sara Calhoun Simonds, the present owner's grandmother, who grew up in the 1890s.

After being in the hands of a family cousin for many years, the home was acquired by its present owners. The house was then renovated and opened as the 1843 Battery Carriage House Inn in 1992.

As you might have guessed, a house with so much history is bound to have a few spirits lurking around. In fact, guests of the 1843 Battery Carriage House Inn have reported so many ghostly encounters, the owners have started recording them. So far, they report, the encounters center around two entities known as the "gentleman ghost" and the "headless torso."

The gentleman ghost, who seems to prefer the single ladies, is thought to be the spirit of a young man whose family owned the house earlier in the century. A sensitive and well-read college student, the man committed suicide by jumping from the roof of the house. Some say he found out that his best friend had married his girl. They reason that he's on his best behavior because he has come back to look for a wife.

No one is quite sure who—or what—the headless torso is. The owners say it's a misnomer to call it headless. They believe it does, indeed, have a head. It's just usually shrouded in darkness, so the spirit is perceived as headless. Judging from the clothing he wears, and considering that the house was built in 1843, after most pirates were banished, they speculate that he's a soldier from the Civil War. He seems to be an unfriendly spirit as well. So far, he's been seen only in Room 8.

Not long after the owners decided to record guests' reports, they were contacted by Paul and Pam, a couple who had stayed in Room 8 a year earlier. After much debate, they said, they were coming forward to report a strange incident that had happened to them during their stay.

It began on their walk back to the inn from the restaurant where they'd had dinner. On that walk, they noticed an inordinate number of cats along the way. There were cats everywhere—lying on the ground in front of them, slinking around every corner, and strolling through lawns. It was a veritable kitty convention. When they later mentioned this to a psychic friend, she told them that cats have an affinity for the spiritual world and that a number of them will appear to someone about to have a ghostly encounter.

The incident happened to Paul during the middle of the night. Ensconced in the antique bed, he was sleeping on his side, facing the wall. He suddenly became aware of a sensation of being watched. He was still asleep, he said, but what was happening was too real to be a dream. He said he could see someone standing next to the bed, and since the antique bed was higher than normal, what he could see without raising his head was just the torso of a very large, barrel-chested man. If there was a head, it was shrouded in darkness. The same was true for the feet and legs. The apparition wore several layers of clothing, with the top layer being some type of outer wear with no buttons—a cape perhaps. This outer garment was made of a type of rough material. When Paul reached out to feel it, rubbing it between his thumb and forefinger, it felt rough and scratchy, like burlap. It was this sensation of touch, he said, that helped to convince him this was more than a dream.

That, and the fact that he could hear raspy breathing, as if the apparition were suffering from allergies.

When Paul touched the coat, the breathing deepened into a threatening moan, as if the apparition were warning him that he didn't want to be touched. At this point, he experienced a feeling of fear, as if the apparition were about to do some harm to him. He tried to scream but was unable to. He kept struggling and finally croaked out a small sound, which brought him to full consciousness. The apparition was gone.

Although he admits to being asleep throughout the incident, Paul was convinced it was more than a dream. The apparition, he said, was a tough customer, someone he wouldn't want to meet in an alley on a dark night or in a quiet bedroom on a dark night.

It's a much different entity that inhabits the inn's Room 10. In late 1992, the owners received a letter concerning the stay of DS and DC, twin sisters who stayed in Room 10 on May 19, 1992. When the sisters retired for the evening, DC placed a chair in front of the door, telling her sister that it would serve as a barrier against intruders. Well, the corporeal ones anyway.

The sisters were sleeping in the same bed, with DC on the left side and DS on the right, facing the door. DC fell asleep almost immediately, but DS was restless, and she lay staring at the doorway. Suddenly, she noticed a wispy gray apparition floating through the door. It floated on through her chair barrier and as it entered, she found that it was the configuration of a man. No facial features were visible and she was unable to discern any clothing, but she was sure it was the figure of a slightly-built man, about 5'8" tall.

As DS watched him, he glided in an upright position over to the bed and lay down in the small space between her and the edge of the bed. He placed his right arm over her shoulders. She didn't feel the pressure of his arm. Neither did she feel frightened or threatened.

Wishing to share the experience with her sister, DS quietly called her name. She called her several times before DC finally awoke and asked what was wrong. When DS spoke up to answer her, the apparition disappeared. She was disappointed that he had left and speculated that he was disturbed by the renovations of the house. She thought he might be looking for a quiet place to get some rest and was hoping they'd be obliged to share their bed. She ended her letter with a wish to return someday to see if her "Gentleman Visitor" would come to call again.

Another encounter with the gentleman ghost occurred in March 2004. The couple had spent a pleasant, but uneventful, night in Room 10. The next day, while the husband was downstairs inquiring on local attractions, the wife was relaxing in bed. Out of the corner of her eye, she caught a shadow going by the window, and when she turned to look, she saw it was the shadow of a man about 5'11" to six feet tall. The shadow passed into the room by the bed and settled onto the closet door, before finally fading. She smelled a clean soap smell as the shadow went past. She assumed it was her husband coming back, but after several minutes, when he didn't enter the room she got up and looked out the door. No one was there.

When her husband came back, she told him of the incident. He went outside to see if someone passing by the window would cast a shadow into the room. Nada. They were intrigued, but clueless. Until they toured Charleston's Old Exchange Building. There in the gift shop, they found a book about the ghosts of

Charleston and read about the gentleman ghost of the Carriage House Inn. Stunned, the wife said she was honored to have been visited by such a famous spirit.

Room 3 is another Carriage House Inn room that seems to be quite supernaturally active. A couple spending a weekend there in September 2002 experienced a series of uncanny events. First, in the middle of the first night, the husband heard the distinctive musical tones of his cell phone, which he had turned off before going to bed, being turned on.

On that night, both the husband and wife saw a light emanating from the bathroom, an eerie experience, since there is no window or source of light other than the overhead lighting there. They also reported seeing the outlines of figures, a congregation of energy masses moving in and out of the room, they said.

The first night, these energy masses moved in and out of the room quickly. On the second night, the light was centered in the sitting room and the figures, which were of varying sizes, moved around the room slowly, seeming to gather and linger around the bed and the sitting area.

47

On their third day at the inn, the couple ran into a clairvoyant who also was staying there. They told her of their experiences and she visited Room 3, where she said she felt a great energy presence. She ordered the spirits to depart. Consequently, their last night at the inn, the couple reported, was uneventful.

The owners say they've never personally seen the ghosts that haunt their inn, but they believe their guests when they say they've experienced something otherworldly. They're intrigued by the stories, and are, no doubt, grateful that they have earned the inn its place on Charleston's ghostly tour, which seems to be quite a draw for many adventurous ghost seekers. Who knew that some day having ghosts in the attic would be a fabulous marketing tool?

Annabel Lee's Return

Annabel Lee's Return

Any high school senior is, no doubt, familiar with Edgar Allan Poe's poem, "Annabel Lee." We might not have had the opportunity to read it had Poe, sensing it would be his last, not taken steps to make sure it was known to others. Upon its completion in May of 1849, he sent out several copies to friends, making sure that the work did not die with him. He made mention of it in lectures and finally sold it to *Sartain's Union Magazine of Literature and Art.* But it was first printed in the *New York Daily Tribune* on October 9, 1849, four days after Poe's death, rushed into print by Rufus Griswold, who had planned to include it in a volume about American poets and their poetry.

Several of Poe's women friends have claimed to have inspired the work. Most scholars believe it was about his recently deceased wife. Poe's wife, however, was named Virginia and any Charlestonian, aware that Poe spent time in their fair city, knows the poem is based upon a famous Charleston legend.

The Legend of Annabel Lee

"It was many and many a year ago,
　　In a kingdom by the sea,
That a maiden there lived whom you may know
　　By the name of ANNABEL LEE;
And this maiden she lived with no other thought
　　Than to love and be loved by me."

The sailor saw it coming, but things happened so fast there was no time to shout a warning. He saw the woman step from the small shop, her arms overloaded with packages. He saw the group of young boys dash across the street, heedless of anything in their path. Saw one of them slam into her, strewing her packages across the walkway, and kept going, laughing delightedly. The lady let out a surprised cry and stood bewildered, looking down at her scattered packages.

The sailor hurried over and began gathering up the packages.

"Here. Let me help you. Are you all right, Miss?" Looking up at her, he was suddenly struck by her beauty. Long, curling auburn hair framed a heart-shaped face. Her emerald eyes, now sparkling with amusement, were fringed by thick black lashes. Ruby lips curled into a smile.

"Yes, yes, I'm fine. Thank you. I never saw them coming!"

"Little hooligans. They never even slowed down." The sailor had gathered up her packages and was standing beside her, his arms full. "Let me help. I'll carry your packages for you."

"Oh, thank you. I really could use the help. I'm already late and my father is waiting. He's going to be upset."

"We can't have that, can we, Miss….?"

She smiled at him again. "Annabel Lee."

"Well, let's go then, Miss Annabel Lee."

They hurried through town toward her home and, as worried as she was about the ire of her father at her lateness, Annabel Lee couldn't help but steal glances at the sailor striding along beside her. Charleston was a busy town, and as a port city, it was always full of sailors. She had never paid them any attention before. They were such a rowdy bunch, usually bleary-eyed drunk, congregating on the street, and making rude noises as she—or any other woman—passed by.

But this one was different. He was so polite and

very handsome, with dark hair and deep dimples when he smiled. He had a wonderful voice, too. It was deep with a soft drawl. Even though their time together was short, she was able to find out that he was from Virginia and that he wasn't just a sailor, he was an officer—a lieutenant—and was hoping to increase his rank soon. He was stationed in Charleston, and he wanted to call on her tomorrow night. She was elated, but cautious. Her father could be such a snob sometimes, but maybe, just maybe, he would be impressed by this gallant, polite soldier.

When they arrived at her home, the sailor took in an audible breath. It wasn't just a home; it was a mansion. Obviously, Miss Annabel Lee was wealthy, and he wondered about his request to call on her. No doubt, she would never be interested in a poor man like him.

Just as they ascended the veranda steps, the front door jerked open and an older man stepped out.

"Annabel Lee! Where have you been? You should have been home by now."

"I'm sorry, Father. I had to wait for the order at the grocery. It took longer than I'd planned. Then, as I came out of the shop with all my parcels, a group of ruffians knocked into me and scattered everything in the street. This nice young sailor was the only one who would stop to help."

The man looked the sailor over with a superior expression. He nodded curtly, taking the packages from him. "Thank you for helping my daughter," he said and turned away. "Annabel, come inside."

As he disappeared into the house, Annabel Lee turned to the young sailor and smiled brightly. "I apologize for my father's rudeness. He was just worried about me."

"Think nothing of it. So, Miss Annabel Lee, have you considered my question? May I call on you tomorrow?"

Casting a glance backward to be sure her father wasn't listening, she replied, "Actually, I was planning another shopping trip tomorrow. Perhaps we could meet in front of the shop where you so graciously helped me."

His dimpled smile sent a shiver through her. "I'll see you there. Say, around noon? Perhaps we can have a picnic lunch in the park."

"Yes! That would be very nice. I'll see you then." After a quick smile, she turned and hurried into the house.

"I was a child and she was a child,
      In this kingdom by the sea,
But we loved with a love that was more than
            love—
      I and my ANNABEL LEE;
With a love that the winged seraphs of heaven
      Coveted her and me."

The next day, Annabel Lee met with her handsome
sailor in front of the shop. The two strolled around the
park, and enjoyed a lovely picnic lunch by the lake. It
took only that short afternoon for both of them to fall
in love. They began to meet every afternoon after the
sailor finished his duties. Each day, Annabel Lee would
leave her house and meet him in town. They would
while away the hours, looking deep into each other's
eyes and speaking sweet words to each other. With
each passing day, they fell more deeply in love.

The only problem in the sweetest situation of
Annabel Lee's life was that she was deceiving her father.
She knew without asking that he would never approve
of her new love and that he would forbid her to ever
see him again. So she made up excuses to be away from
home. But, of course, one day the inevitable happened.

"Annabel Lee! What are you doing with this man? You said you were lunching with friends."

"Father!"

"You come with me right now, miss! I will not have you consorting with a mere soldier. You are finer than that."

"But, Father, I…"

"Come along. You must obey me."

Without a word to the sailor, and with Annabel Lee in tears, he dragged her home. For days, he kept a close watch on her, not allowing her to leave the house for any reason. She sat in her room, looking out the window toward the harbor, where she knew her love to be. It was a miserable time, but then one day her father announced that he had to leave town on business. He would be gone for two weeks, he said, and he strictly forbade her to see that sailor while he was gone.

"And this was the reason that, long ago,
    In this kingdom by the sea,
A wind blew out of a cloud, chilling
    My beautiful ANNABEL LEE;
So that her high-born kinsman came

56

> And bore her away from me,
> To shut her up in sepulchre,
>   In this kingdom by the sea."

Her father had barely left town, when Annabel summoned her maid. She handed her a letter and told her to whom she should deliver it. Then she left the house through the back door. Winding her way through the nearby wooded area, she came upon the cemetery of the Unitarian Church, where she found a bench in a shady area. She sat there in the coolness of a big oak, her heart in her throat, terrified that he wouldn't come; afraid that in the short time they had been apart, his heart had changed and he'd found someone else.

But his heart had not changed. He was still very much in love. He rushed to the cemetery as soon as he read her note, happy, at last, to hear from her.

"My love!" Annabel ran to him. "I was so afraid you wouldn't come!"

"Nay, my beautiful Annabel Lee. I could not stay away. These days without you have been endless. I was afraid I'd never see you again."

Again, the couple began to meet daily, the

Unitarian Church cemetery becoming their special place. They strolled among the gravestones, oblivious to the irony of a love growing so strongly in the land of the dead. For almost two glorious weeks, they were happy.

On the day before Annabel Lee's father was scheduled to return, they met in the early afternoon. Aware of the short time they had left, they were making plans to elope. The next day, the sailor was scheduled for leave. They made plans to meet that next morning, before the city began to stir. They would travel to the sailor's home state of Virginia, where they would be married. They would, of course, have to return to Charleston until the sailor received his next promotion, when he would be transferred, but after they were married, Annabel Lee was sure that her father would accept their relationship.

Unbeknownst to the couple, however, Annabel's father had returned early. When he entered the house and found her gone, he roughly questioned the young maid, who cracked under the pressure. She told him where he could find his daughter.

Her father stormed to the cemetery and found his daughter in the arms of the handsome sailor. In his anger, he grabbed his daughter's arm, and, despite protests from both, he dragged her roughly home. Shutting her up in her room once again, he refused to allow her to leave and, ignoring repeated attempts from the sailor, refused to allow the couple to see each other.

Weeks passed, the sailor received his promotion and, just as expected, was transferred back to Virginia. He wrote letter after letter, only to have each one returned unopened. Finally, months later, he learned from friends in Charleston that his beautiful Annabel Lee had died of yellow fever.

> "The angels, not half so happy in heaven,
>   Went envying her and me—
> Yes! —That was the reason (as all men know,
>   In this kingdom by the sea)
> That the wind came out of the cloud by night
>   Chilling and killing my ANNABEL LEE.
>
> "But our love it was stronger by far than the love
>   Of those who were older than we—
>   Of many far wiser than we—
> And neither the angels in Heaven above,

> Nor the demons down under the sea,
> Can ever dissever my soul from the soul
>   Of the beautiful ANNABEL LEE."

The sailor rushed to Charleston only to find that his beautiful Annabel Lee had been laid to rest in their former trysting place, the Unitarian Church cemetery. Not wanting the sailor to know where to grieve, her father, a vindictive sort, had dug his daughter's grave to six feet, but also re-dug his relatives' graves to three feet, not far enough to disturb their rest, but far enough to camouflage Annabel Lee's grave.

It didn't matter to the grief-stricken sailor. Everyday he came and sat beside the family plot, weeping for his lost love. He sat for hours, sometimes late into the night, dreaming of the happy days spent in that very cemetery—the happiest days of his life, with his beautiful Annabel Lee.

> "For the moon never beams, without bringing me
>   dreams
>   Of the beautiful ANNABEL LEE;
> And the stars never rise, but I feel the bright eyes
>   Of the beautiful ANNABEL LEE:

And so, all the night-tide, I lie down by the side
Of my darling—my darling—my life and my bride,
    In her sepulchre there by the sea,
    In her tomb by the sounding sea."

According to legend, the beautiful Annabel Lee still walks among the living. Her spirit has been sighted strolling disconsolately through the Unitarian Church cemetery. Many Charlestonians believe she walks there among the gravestones, searching for her lost sailor.

The Lighthouses of
South Carolina

The Lighthouses of South Carolina

For centuries, lighthouses were beacons that saved many a ship from certain doom on the shoals of South Carolina's coast. The people who manned the lighthouses were dedicated. They knew that to keep the lighthouse lamp lit was to save lives.

With today's sophisticated navigational equipment, the lighthouses are now a beautiful part of history. But according to legend, a couple of South Carolina's lighthouses are still manned by spirits from the past, who haven't gotten the word that their efforts are no longer needed.

The Blue Lady of Hilton Head

It was August 30, 1898, and word was a vicious hurricane was bearing down on Hilton Head Island. Already the wind was whipping sand into painful swirls that pelted lighthouse master Adam Fripp as he made his way around the lighthouse, securing the grounds.

Fripp had been the keeper of Hilton Head's lighthouse since it was put into operation in 1884. It

64

was actually the second lighthouse built on the spot. The first had been set atop the keeper's house and rose to a height of only thirty-five feet. This height was impossibly short, considering that the island's passage channel was ever shifting.

To alleviate the problem, a ninety-five-foot range-light lighthouse had been erected behind the original. This new, taller lighthouse was constructed of steel in a skeletal style around a solid cylinder. It was mobile, which meant it could be moved around as the channel moved. Now that there were two lighthouses, a range-light system was being used. A large Fresnel light, which could be seen fifteen miles out to sea, was placed on the mobile light house, and a smaller light was placed in the short lighthouse. By aligning the two lights, sailors could safely navigate the hazards around the island.

Despite its spindly appearance, the skeletal lighthouse tower was built to withstand gales and hurricanes. Fripp felt safe enough riding out the storm here, and he knew it was essential that the beacon stay lit, beaming its warning out to the hapless sailors caught in the storm. Keeping the light going could well save lives and that was his job. So there was no question that he was staying.

"Father! Father! Where are you?"

At the sound of his daughter's voice, Fripp rounded the corner of the keeper's house.

"Caroline! What are you doing here? The storm is coming ashore now! You should be in town."

"I wasn't about to leave you out here by yourself. You might need help keeping the light going with the wind so high."

Caroline was his youngest daughter and he doted on her. She'd always been a daddy's girl, dogging his every footstep as a toddler and wrapping him around her teenage finger. Now at twenty-one, she was a beautiful young woman who still enjoyed spending time with her old father. He should've known she'd be worried and come out here.

The wind was coming in harder now. Trees were beginning to bend over and objects were flying through the air.

"Get inside!" Fripp screamed to Caroline. He followed her into the lighthouse, both struggling with the door to shut it against the howling wind.

"Get out the checkers and make us some coffee," he said. "I'm going up to check the lantern."

About halfway up the tight spiral staircase, Fripp

was breathing hard. He began feeling a tightness in his chest. At the top, he paused for a moment to catch his breath. It was just fatigue, he told himself. He hadn't slept well last night, worrying about the coming storm. That's all it was.

Striding into the lantern room, he made his checks quickly. Everything was shipshape. He had turned to go, when suddenly there was a loud crashing sound and glass began splintering down. Something had crashed into the lantern! It was shattered and the wind howled into the tiny room, extinguishing the kerosene lamp that was so vital to the sailors.

As he turned back toward the room, an excruciating pain squeezed his chest and radiated down his left arm. Struggling for breath, he tried to make it over to the lamp. He had to re-light it! The pain in his chest worsened. It was squeezing the breath out of him. He collapsed onto the floor, clutching at his chest and gasping for air.

Suddenly, Caroline was by his side. "Father! What's wrong? Are you hurt?"

"No," he gasped out. "My chest is hurting. Caroline, you've got to re-light the lantern! It's imperative. You've got to light it and keep it lit."

"But, Father, What about you? I've got to go for help!"

"No!" He grabbed her wrist. "You can't leave. I'll be all right. Just get the lamp lit. Go." He pushed her hands away. "Go!"

Caroline reluctantly stood and headed toward the lamp. She had spent most of her childhood here, helping her father with his duties. She knew how to light the lamp. The problem was going to be keeping it lit with the wind blowing through.

"Caroline," her father called her back momentarily. "Promise me, Daughter. Promise me that no matter what happens, you'll keep the lamp lit. There are sailors out there in this storm. Without the light to show them the dangers, they'll run aground. They could drown. If the light's lit, they at least have a chance to steer clear. Now, promise me you'll keep it lit!"

Tears streamed down her face. "I promise, Daddy. I promise I will."

Caroline returned to the lamp and, with great difficulty, got it lit.

"It's lit, Father!" There was no answer. "Father!" As soon as she turned away, the wind blew the lamp out again. Caroline was torn. She wanted desperately to go to her father; to go get help for him. But she had promised. She knew how dedicated her father was to his responsibilities. She had promised she would keep the lamp lit, and she knew she had to keep that promise.

All through the long, dark, and windy night, Caroline kept her vigil, sheltering the lamp so that it could beam its warning beacon out to sea. She would call out to her father, but there was never a response. Still, she stayed at the lamp, faithfully keeping her promise to her father.

Finally, morning broke. Heavy clouds still blanketed the sky, but the wind was finally still. Exhausted, Caroline left her post at the lamp and rushed to her father's side, but one look told her it was too late. Her father had died during the night.

Caroline was devastated. She was hailed as a hero for her efforts in keeping the lighthouse lamp lit. Because of her, several ships had been saved. But she believed that had she left and gotten help, her father would still be alive. Her grief would not let her rest. Every night afterward, she would have nightmares about that long night, with her father lying dead on the floor. It was more than she could take, and within weeks, she, too, had died. She was buried in a beautiful blue gown.

The short front lighthouse was decommissioned in 1932 and was later destroyed. The tall skeletal construction lighthouse was deactivated in 1930s, but remains in good condition today. It sits at the Palmetto Dunes Resort on Hilton Head Island, along with the oil house and a cistern.

According to legend, Caroline, dressed in her blue gown, faithfully keeps her promise to her father to this day. She's been seen wandering the grounds around the lighthouse, and there have been numerous reports of the sound of a woman crying coming from inside the lighthouse, especially on stormy nights.

Little Annie of Winyah Bay

Georgetown, named in honor of King George I, was founded in 1729 and became an official port of entry in 1732. Within a few years it had become a major commerce center. Prior to that, all foreign imports and exports had to pass through Charleston. By the time of the American Revolution, hundreds of acres of cypress swamp land had been cleared and more than 780 miles had been dug, making the area the world's second largest rice cultivation center. Georgetown also was a center for the cultivation of Indigo, which is used to make blue dye.

Ships trading in these two commodities had to sail between North and South Islands to enter Winyah Bay, then sail up the river into Georgetown, a sometimes treacherous route because of the rocky shoals. Although the land for placement of a lighthouse on North Island was donated by Revolutionary War patriot Paul Trapier in 1789, it was more than a decade before the lighthouse was finally built. The seventy-two-foot cypress wood tower was erected in 1801, during the last days of John Adams's presidency. In addition to the tower, there was a two-story keeper's house and a large tank for holding the whale oil that

71

was used to light the lighthouse lamp. The lighthouse had been erected only five years when a massive storm toppled it.

It was 1811 before the lighthouse was replaced, this time with a seventy-two-foot sturdy brick building that would not so easily succumb to storms. There is a stone stairway that spirals inside the lighthouse and in 1857, a Fresnel lens was added.

During the Civil War, the lighthouse was used as a lookout point for Confederates, but then it was captured by Union troops. The war played havoc with its exterior, and as part of the post-war repair, it was lengthened to eighty-seven feet.

The lighthouse was manned until 1986, when the Coast Guard installed an automated light. A solar-powered system was installed in 1999. The lighthouse was used for a short time as a juvenile detention center, but then was placed on the National Registry of Historic Places, a move that may see it restored to its original condition.

In addition to the solar-powered beacon beaming from the lighthouse to warn them away from the shoals, the sailors of Georgetown also have a hurricane warning system. Her name is Annie.

Back in the early 1800s, weather forecasting was pretty much your-best-guess-is-as-good-as-mine. In those days, sudden and violent storms would slam into the island with no warning. It was at this time that pretty, fair-haired Annie lived at the lighthouse with its keeper, her father.

Since there was nothing on the island but the lighthouse, Annie and her father would row across Winyah Bay into Georgetown for supplies. Annie's father would always plan their trips by the tides, and they would always return before evening in order to light the lighthouse's whale-oil beacon.

On one glorious morning, Annie's father had awakened and decided it would be a good day for a trip across the bay for supplies. The sun had been shining brightly, and there wasn't a cloud to be seen. They had rowed over to Georgetown early that morning, and had spent a pleasant day shopping and visiting with friends. Annie's father had been enjoying himself so much he hadn't noticed that the wind had freshened and that a bank of clouds was moving over the bay. And they had left later than planned.

Now, as he was rowing strenuously against a swift current, rain began pelting down and the wind suddenly began gusting, kicking up waves that splashed into their small boat. He glanced at the bow of the boat. Annie was clinging to her seat, a look of fear on her sweet little face. The wind grew stronger, and the waves became taller and more threatening. The boat tossed side to side, at the mercy of the raging water. Annie and her father were in a desperate situation, but it was too late to turn back. They were closer to the island than to Georgetown.

Suddenly, a huge gust of wind drove a wave over the boat, swamping it. Annie screamed and her father grabbed her as they both ended up in the choppy water. Taking one of the boat lines, he quickly lashed her onto his back and began swimming toward shore. Reaching it, he crawled out of the surf and collapsed.

When he awoke many hours later, he had no recollection of the terror they had encountered. He did not remember strapping the child to his back, or crawling to shore. He was brought abruptly into reality, however, when he found Annie still lashed to his back. Sadly, she had not made it. She had drowned before they reached shore.

Since that time—even until today—sailors have reported seeing the spirit of a beautiful blonde child.

According to legend, she appears on boats plying the water of the bay. She usually appears on a bright, sunny day, pointing back to shore and pleading for the sailors to go back. The sailors ignore her warning at their own peril. The legend says those who keep sailing soon find themselves in a furious storm and may well end up in a watery grave.

The Ghosts of Camden

The Ghosts of Camden

Camden may not have Charleston's reputation as the country's most haunted city, but this little town has its fair share of haunting spirits—and with good reason. Camden is South Carolina's oldest inland town. First established as Fredricksburg in 1732, it disappeared after only a few years. Another township, named Pine Tree Hill, was established in 1758. It was renamed Camden in honor of Lord Camden, a champion of colonial rights named Charles Pratt. With such a long a rich history, it's no wonder Camden is a spirited town.

Camden's Gray Lady

The spirit world sure is colorful. In just this collection of stories alone, there's a Gray Lady, along with the Gray Man, plus the Blue Lady. I've found that almost every state in the union has at least one Lady in White, and in North Carolina I've even encountered a Pink Lady. Maybe latching onto the color of their clothes makes it easier for us to accept their otherworldliness. And then again maybe it's just an easy way to describe them!

Camden's Gray Lady could also be described as the French Lady. According to accounts from the Camden Archives and Museum, this particular Gray Lady is the spirit of Eloise DeSaurin, who lived in France in the 1500s. She was a young woman and like most young women, she believed in following her heart, even when she knew her heart was leading her into trouble.

See, Eloise had fallen in love with a handsome young French Huguenot. A devout Catholic, her father, Darce, hated Huguenots—had, indeed, banished his own sons for their Huguenot sentiments. He forbade his daughter to see the young man of her dreams, but Eloise, being very much in love and a bit headstrong to boot, ignored the order. The two would meet as often as possible for titillating trysts in a secret hideaway.

Unfortunately, their hideaway wasn't such a secret, and one fateful day, her father caught them together. Furious, he drew his dagger and charged the young man. Darce was a burly guy, and could have easily killed the man, but Eloise stepped between them.

Tearfully, she begged her father to spare her love.

She swore she'd never see him again, if, please, please, he could just let him go in peace. Coming to his senses, Darce sheathed his dagger and let the young man go, but he wasn't falling for that "I'll never see him again" trick. He'd already been fooled once. This time he was taking no chances.

That very week, he packed up his daughter and shipped her off to a convent, an unwise act that brought much tragedy to Darce and his family. Eloise, stuck away in the convent, fell into a deep depression. Her heart was broken. Not only had she lost the love of her life, but she also had lost her family. Alone and lonely, she began to pine away, and within a couple of years, she died. Blaming Darce for Eloise's death, her mother lost her mind and soon followed her daughter in death.

Riddled with guilt and saddened by the loss he'd caused his family, Darce contacted his estranged sons. He told them that their sister's spirit had visited him and had sternly reproached him for what he had done. He wanted to make things right with them before he died, he said. Then, drawing the same dagger with which he'd threatened the young Huguenot, he plunged it into his chest.

The sons lived in the house for several years without incident. France was in religious turmoil, however, which was about to culminate in an attempted purge of Huguenots in the country. In August 1572, the anguished spirit of Eloise appeared to her brother Raoul. She was silent, but he could tell she was upset about something.

That night, he found a monk's outfit in his room. Several days later, on August 24, dressed in the monk's garb, he escaped death in the massacre of St. Bartholomew's Day, in which tens of thousands of Huguenots were slaughtered for their beliefs.

That was the last sighting of Eloise in France. Perhaps she decided to do as many others before her and immigrate to a country whose constitution was based on religious freedom. Whatever the reason, it soon became apparent that Eloise had come to South Carolina when a relative, Maj. John McPherson DeSaussure, bought a home in Camden, a home he called Lausanne.

According to museum archives, Eloise appeared to people to warn them of impending doom. In one of her most famous sightings, she appeared to Camden citizen Nina Beaumont, a DeSaussure relative, who was a houseguest at Lausanne at the time of the sighting. Seems Beaumont was having problems sleeping one night. She got up and walked out into the hallway where she saw Eliose's spirit.

Knowing Eloise's penchant of warning of danger, Beaumont begged her fiancé to drop his plans for hunting the next day. He, of course, thought the whole thing was nonsense. He kept his hunting plans and was accidentally shot and killed.

By the 1940s, Lausanne had been turned into a bed and breakfast called the Court Inn. According to Arthur Slade III, who lived at the inn as a child, his mother related another Gray Lady story. There was a fire in the inn one night in the 1940s, and Slade's mother told him she was trying to save the old grandfather clock. She said the ceiling fell, barely missing her, and when she looked up on the landing, she saw the Gray Lady standing there, holding the grandfather clock. Luckily, Slade's mother escaped the fire and was able to tell her ghost story.

The old Court Inn was torn down in 1964, and since that time, the Gray Lady spirit of Eloise DeSaurin has not been seen since. Her legend, however, lives on in the streets of Camden.

Agnes of Glasgow

"Agnes, my love. I will return, I promise. I love you. Please don't cry."

Those had been Lt. Angus Pherson's last words to her as he boarded the military ship bound for America. He'd been called to duty to fight for the British in the war going on in the New World.

Agnes hadn't been able to help herself, however. She had cried bitterly as her love departed. She loved him so, and the idea of being parted from him was almost unbearable. America was so far away from their Scottish homeland. She'd lived day to day, anxiously awaiting his letters. Weeks dragged into months and now it had been more than a year—a truly, truly miserable year. Still there was no word of Angus's return.

Agnes decided she could wait no longer. If he couldn't come home to her, then she'd go to him. She'd gone down to the docks of Glasgow and searched out a kindly sea captain, one who seemed to be a bit of a romantic at heart. Her tears and plaintive pleas had obviously touched him, and he'd agreed to give her passage to America.

That's what she was doing, standing on the deck of

this leaky ship, taking in her first look at the land called America. The ship was getting ready to dock in a town called Charleston, the town where Angus was stationed, at least according to her last letter. That letter had been weeks ago, and Agnes was worried that Angus was no longer here, but she'd find out where he was. She'd come this far, and she was determined that she would find him. She couldn't wait to see his handsome face, a face she'd so desperately missed these many months.

The ship docked and Agnes excitedly gathered her things. A quick carriage ride later, and she was inside the bustling town of Charleston. It was so big and busy! She'd expected it to be primitive, with few buildings or people. But this was a metropolis, not unlike her hometown of Glasgow. Its obvious civilization enheartened her. Surely, she'd be able to find Angus here!

She went straight to the British camp and begged a meeting with the officer in charge, a pompous old man who seemed put out by her presence here.

"Yes, of course I know Lieutenant McPherson. But, really, miss, this is most unusual." He said. "He never mentioned to me that you would be coming to America."

"That's because he doesn't know." Agnes's hands twisted nervously in her lap. "I didn't tell him what I was planning. I just could wait no longer. He's been gone for more than a year. I would think you'd be through with this silly war by now, but it just keeps dragging on. I had to see him, so I decided to come here."

"I'm sorry we were unable to finish this 'silly' war on your schedule, miss. However, as I said, this is most unusual. And I have no time to babysit one of my officer's lovers. I'll have someone take you to an inn."

"No! I want to see Angus. I've come this far, and I'll not be deterred. Tell me where he is, please, sir. I must see him."

The look he gave her made Agnes nervous. At first he seemed about to refuse her request, but then his look changed to one of sympathy.

"What is it, sir? Has something happened to Angus?"

"I'm afraid so, miss. I received word yesterday that McPherson was wounded in battle two days ago. He's at a hospital in Camden."

"Camden? Where is that? I must go there."

"That is impossible. The roads are constantly

patrolled by the Continentals, and I have no one to escort you there. The only other way is by river and the only people who'd be able to get you there are the Indians who live just outside of town."

"Oh! Then that's what I have to do. I'll find those Indians and get them to take me to Camden."

Agnes was a determined woman and, more, she was a determined woman in love. She found someone in town to take her to the Indians, and using the jewelry and trinkets she had brought with her, she bartered for passage by canoe to Camden. As they glided down the river, edged by wilderness on both sides, Agnes became anxious. The wilderness was dense and probably held all kinds of dangers, from Continentals to fearsome beasts. She was afraid, but she had to get to Angus. She had to continue on in this dark world.

The trip took two endless days, but finally the Indians put into shore and indicated that they had reached their destination. They pointed Agnes in the direction toward Camden, then launched their canoes back into the river.

The trek to town through dense forest was terrifying. Agnes was exhausted. She hadn't slept in days and had barely had anything to eat. She felt weak and sick, but she pressed on. Finally, at almost dark, she reached the outskirts of town. She grabbed the first passerby.

"Please, sir, I must find the British military hospital. Can you show it to me?"

The man looked at the disheveled girl. Her hair was all matted, and she was dirty. She did, in fact, look in need of a hospital, so he pointed it out to her.

As she entered the hospital, she stopped a nurse.

"Please, I must see Lieutenant Angus McPherson. I've come all the way from Scotland. Please take me to him."

The nurse placed a hand on her shoulder. "I'm sorry, miss. Lt. McPherson died just moments ago. I was with him when he passed. He went quietly."

"No! No! That can't be!" Agnes began running through the hospital, searching each bed for her love. Finally finding him, she threw herself across him. "Oh, Angus! My sweet love! I've missed you so." She stroked his face, tears streaming from her eyes. "I've come this far to see you. You can't leave me now!"

But, indeed, Angus was gone. Agnes was so heartbroken at losing her handsome lieutenant she fell ill and died.

The tragic story of Agnes of Glasgow is detailed on a marker in the old Presbyterian churchyard near Kershaw County's Quaker cemetery, and her story is told in the Camden Archives and Museum. Legend has it that the lettering on her tombstone was etched by a soldier's bayonet.

Although the veracity of Agnes's story is doubted by historians who say the British didn't come to Camden until months after Agnes died, Camden citizens don't doubt. For on many occasions through the centuries, the apparition of a young woman has been seen forlornly wandering the streets of the town.

The Headless Horseman of Hobkirk Hill

The story of Camden's headless horseman is a gruesome tale that has some basis in fact. Historians agree that such an incident occurred during the Battle of Hobkirk Hill.

At that point, Camden was a key British base, and American Major General Nathanial Greene was sent with a contingent of fifteen hundred to capture it. They were camped on Hobkirk Hill on April 25, 1781, when British General Lord Francis Rawdon staged a surprise attack.

Greene was caught by surprise, but the discipline he had drilled into his men proved valuable. He was able to quickly muster a force of 930 into battle and defend his position.

The battle was fierce and the Americans fought valiantly. According to legend, during the heat of battle, an American solider was charging through the battlefield on his trusty steed, when a cannonball sailed through the air and hit him, severing his head from his body.

The soldier's horse was unharmed, and it charged off with the soldier still in the saddle, disappearing into the swamp near Black River Road. The battle raged on and, despite their valiant effort, the Americans were forced to retreat. It wasn't a complete defeat, however. The damage they inflicted upon the British resulted in their subsequent abandonment of Camden, a vital move that helped the Continentals to eventually take South Carolina.

It wasn't long after the battle that reports began circulating around Camden about a strange apparition haunting the battlefield. The apparition was that of a soldier mounted on a charging horse, kind of your everyday ghost story, except for one thing: The

89

horseman has lost his head—literally. Legend has it that the headless horseman can be seen on foggy nights, especially when the moon is full. He wanders the battlefield—searching for his head no doubt. He disappears before daylight. Although historians agree that such an incident did occur during the Battle of Hobkirk Hill, they're not sure if it was an American or a British solider that lost his head. Either way, it makes a great story to tell around the campfire!

The Little Person of Beaufort

The Little Person of Beaufort

Beaufort has a little ghost story. Actually, it's the ghost that's little. The story is big and is one of the state's oldest.

According to legend, the story began back in February 1562. That year, French Naval officer Jean Ribaut was sent to America with two ships containing a group of 150 Huguenots. They were sailing for Florida to establish a colony. It wasn't until April 30 that the ships reached the east coast of Florida somewhere near Anastasia Island. Sailing north along the coast, they entered the River May—now the St. John's River—on May 1.

The group spent a few days here, near what's now Jacksonville. They met with the local Indians, explored the river, and erected a stone monument to establish the French claim on the area. For some reason though, Ribaut decided against establishing a colony here. Instead, he and his two ships sailed on north in search of new territory.

On May 17, 1562, they sailed into a large harbor

Ribaut described as "one of the greatest and fayrest [*sic*] havens of the world." He called the harbor Port Royal. After spending several days exploring, he erected another stone monument on a small island, now Parris Island, in Port Royal Sound. It was here that he decided to establish the new colony.

The crew built a small fort on the east side of the island and Ribaut named the place Charlesfort. A large house of wood and earth with a straw roof was constructed to serve as a storehouse and barracks. When this was completed, Ribaut named a contingent of twenty-seven men, including gentlemen, soldiers, and mariners, to stay in the new settlement.

Among the colonists was a dwarf named Gauche, who was a jester by trade. He often wore his jester's costume—pointed three-corner hat, brightly patterned coat and pants, and little pointed shoes with bells on the toes. According to reports, Gauche compensated for his size by being a tough customer.

After establishing the colony, Ribaut set sail for France, with the plan to return to Charlesfort in six months with supplies and more settlers. The religious civil war in France put a kink in his plans, however. Ribaut was forced to England and imprisoned as a spy.

93

Meanwhile, back at the settlement, the colonists were running into some hard times. They had not planted crops and a fire had destroyed their supplies. Though many died, the survivors, with the help of the Orista Indians, built a ship and tried to return to France. Their meager supplies ran out quickly and they were forced to eat their leather shoes and jackets. When those delectable treats ran out, the desperate sailors drew lots and dined on the loser before being rescued by an English ship.

The exact fate of Gauche is not known. Some say he died of illness at Charlesfort and, Lord knows, what with the heat, the humidity, and all those bloodthirsty mosquitoes, there was a lot of that going around. Some say he was hanged by a Captain Albert, who must've taken umbrage at one of the jester's pranks. Still others say the dwarf turned out to be the loser of the food lottery aboard the ill-fated return ship—although he would've made a small meal, I'd think.

Whatever his actual fate, the general consensus is that Gauche has taken up residence at one of Beaufort's most beautiful homes. Often called "The Castle" because of the medieval feel of its architecture, the Joseph Johnson House was built in 1861 by Dr. Joseph Fickling

Johnson. It's said to be the exact replica of a house in England, subsequently destroyed in World War II.

The house is built in the Italian Renaissance style, with six massive columns supporting the double portico and balusters between that enclose the upper and lower porches. There is a decorated parapet that is five feet high, with four triple chimneys towering above. Its color is changeable, in shades of gray, tan, and pink that shift subtly with the light.

During the Civil War, the house was occupied by Union troops, who used it as a hospital. The laundry house on the premises served as a morgue. Unlike many of Beaufort's residents, Dr. Johnson was able to reacquire the house after the war by paying $2,000 in taxes. It remained in the family until 1981.

Today, the Joseph Johnson House takes up a full city block on Craven Street. One of the most photographed houses in America, it's surrounded by lush gardens filled with azaleas and camellias. Many of the trees and shrubs were planted by Dr. Johnson, including a pair of olive trees brought from the Mount of Olives in Israel.

Soon after the house was completed in 1861, reports began to surface of a peculiar ghost that lived in the cellar. Gardeners reported seeing a dwarf dressed in jester's clothing wandering the grounds. They would often catch just a glimpse of him as he rounded a corner of the house.

Even Dr. Johnson reported seeing the apparition one night. He said he saw a face peeking through the window at him and, when sighted, it scurried away, laughing hysterically, with the bells on his shoes tinkling a mad tune.

While Johnson's son often sighted the jester, and said he was a "rough customer" who disliked everyone, he must've had a soft spot for little girls. Johnson's little daughter, Lily, reported Gauche would join her in the tea parties she held in the basement of the house. She said he swore a lot. He also liked to play his jester's pranks on houseguests, moving furniture and slamming doors all night along. These sounds were always accompanied by the sound of the tinkling bells on his feet. He's also been known to leave red handprints on upstairs windows.

According to Lily, who in later life reported on her experiences, the family discovered that Gauche was communicating by a code tapped out on tables. They found someone who could translate and learned that he was speaking in archaic sixteenth-century French. A report about a houseguest who interviewed the malevolent Gauche was published in *Tales of Beaufort* by Nell S. Graydon. In the interview, the houseguest asked the spirit his name, to which he replied "Gauche." He said he lived in the cellar of the house because it reminded him of his childhood home that he would never see again. The guest then asked if she could see him, to which he puckishly replied, "No, I do not show myself to fools."

There is another popular story about Gauche, who would seem to be a hungry, wandering spirit. According to legend, in 1969 he wandered across town to the Howard Danner home and stole a roast that Mrs. Danner had left sitting on the stove. She had removed the roast from the oven so that she could take the maid home and when she returned, the roast was gone. The police report speculated that Gauche the ghost had become hungry and had absconded with the roast.

If so, he must've enjoyed it so much that he visited the home of a neighbor the very next night and stole that family's roast dinner, as well. The house, which had been locked, looked undisturbed, except for the missing roast.

Should you visit the Joseph Johnson House, you might just get a glimpse of the jester's ghost. That is, if he doesn't think you're a fool. Maybe bringing a roast would help.

Alice of the Hermitage

Alice of the Hermitage

A hush fell over the ballroom when Miss Alice Flagg appeared at the head of the stairs. Even to the women in the room, her beauty was mesmerizing. She had huge, luminous dark eyes, and her burnished auburn hair fell loosely to her waist. Adorned only by a small diamond necklace, she positively glowed in the soft white gown she was wearing. The hush continued until she had descended the stairs and was met by Dr. Allard Flagg, her older brother. As Allard took her hand and led her into the ballroom, the crowd again erupted into party sounds.

Allard presented his sister to a tall, blonde woman.

"Penelope, may I present to you my sister, Alice. Alice, this is Penelope Ward, my fiancée."

"It's very nice to meet you, Alice. Allard has told me so much about you. Have you and your mother settled in?"

"Yes, we're very happy here, thank you. It was so nice of Allard to invite us to live here. The Hermitage is such a beautiful home, don't you think?"

Allard, who was owner of the family's Wachesaw Plantation, had built the home on Murrell's Inlet just last year—1849. It was to serve as his summer home and the home of Alice and their mother. Alice loved the home, so close to the ocean, and she was happy to be living here.

She was excited by her brother's life here, as well. In the week since they'd arrived, this was the second party he had hosted in their honor. Neither gathering showed any hint of the austerity that the war would bring in a few short years. Elegantly attired young men bowed gallantly before lavishly dressed young women as soft music played in the background.

At age sixteen, Alice welcomed any reason to get dressed up in a fancy ball gown and to dance the night away. She loved the attention, though she was often taken aback by the reaction of other people to her. She had been an awkward, scrawny child and had only blossomed in the last couple of years. She still saw herself as that child and was surprised by the attention her beauty brought.

The reason for this second party had been to introduce her and her mother to Penelope, who had been away when they first arrived. Allard had talked about her incessantly, and Alice had been eager to make her acquaintance.

After their first meeting Alice had circulated a bit, but returned to Penelope, in hopes of getting to know her better. The two had been engaged in small talk for quite some time, and Alice was uncharitably wondering just what Allard was thinking. The woman, though attractive in a horsy sort of way, was thoroughly condescending, spending the entire time pointing out the financial and social foibles of the other guests. Alice was doing her best to be polite, but, frankly, she was bored.

Of course, she did know what Allard was thinking. She knew that the Wards of Brookwood Plantation were the most powerful planters in the Low Country. They cultivated millions of pounds of rice and oats, and thousands of bushels of vegetables every year. They even had a salt making system on the seashore that yielded up to forty bushels of salt daily.

As parishoners of All Saints Episcopal Church at Pawleys Island, the Wards were regarded as examples for others to follow. The rector considered them to be among the most loyal and devoted of his flock. Certainly they were the most accomplished and highly regarded.

They were the elite of South Carolina, wealthy and powerful. And as much as she loved her brother, she knew it was that wealth and power that appealed to him. It was the reason he planned to marry Penelope, despite the fact that she was a boring snob. He valued her social station over love.

That was something Alice could never understand. She valued love over everything. Despite her privileged upbringing, she had never been a snob, had never considered one's social standing as a reason to love or reject. Take, for instance, the man she had met just that very morning while shopping. He was gorgeous. Tall, with dark hair and blue eyes fringed by the longest lashes. So what if he wasn't rich? Or powerful? She didn't care. He was handsome, and sweet, and he seemed to be really interested in her.

She knew neither her brother nor her mother would approve, but she didn't care. She had to follow her heart. She had told him she would meet him in town that next day, and she planned to keep the date.

Little did she know just how much her family would disapprove and to what lengths they would go to stop her budding romance.

The weeks slipped by, with Alice making excuses to go into town as often as possible. There, she would meet with her handsome beau and they would stroll down to the beach, talking and laughing. By the middle of the summer, they had fallen deeply in love, and Alice was in a quandary. She knew she had to introduce him to her family, but she dreaded it. She knew they, in their snobbery, would look down their noses at him, a lowly turpentine merchant. Finally, though, she could put it off no longer. She told him to call on her at the Hermitage the next day.

Alice was up at first light the next morning. She spent more time than usual dressing for breakfast, carefully curling her hair and choosing just the right frock. Her mother and brother were already seated at the table when she appeared. Deciding to broach the subject right away, she nervously took a cup of coffee and sat.

"Umm…Allard, I just wanted to let you know that I will be having some company today. A young man has asked to call on me, and I've invited him over for tea this afternoon."

Allard gave her a wary look. "Well, of course, you may have callers, Alice, but who is this young man and why haven't you spoken of him?"

"He's a prosperous shop owner, Allard, a very nice man. I like him and I hope that you will, too."

"A merchant? You've invited a mere shop owner to call on you here? At the Hermitage? I won't hear of it!"

Angry, Alice rose. "You won't hear of it? Honestly, Allard. Listen to yourself! How can you be such a snob?"

"Alice, you are a Flagg. You must see that a merchant is below your station. Do you want to spend the rest of your life in squalor?"

"There is nothing wrong with loving a man who actually works for a living. Can't you see it's what's inside that matters, not how much money you have or your 'social station'?"

"I'll hear no more. My word is final. Mother, you'll take Alice with you to Georgetown this morning. I'll handle her caller."

"Of course, dear. Alice, go get ready. We'll be leaving in an hour."

Despite Alice's pleading and crying, Allard refused

to change his mind. He sent her off with her mother, and, meeting the young man at the front gate, quickly dispatched him back to town. If he thought that was the end of the situation, however, he was mistaken.

Defiant of her family's wishes, Alice continued to see her young man secretly. Each time she was with him, she fell more deeply in love, and she knew he felt the same. She knew if her family would just get to know him they, too, would love him. After several more weeks, she once again invited him to call on her at the Hermitage. They would take a buggy ride, she said. Surely, once Allard saw her determination, he would relent.

This time she did not mention the young man's impending visit. Instead, she carefully dressed and sat in the window of her bedroom until she saw his buggy, pulled by a pair of sleek bays, coming up the lane. She hurried down the stairs and out to the veranda, a smile lighting her face as she watched the buggy pull up. Her young man helped her into the buggy, and they were about to pull away, when Allard rushed down the veranda.

"Wait!"

Alice urged her beau to go on, but, not wanting to make matters worse, he stopped the buggy.

Allard imperiously pulled the young man from the buggy.

"I have ordered my horse brought around. I'll ride in the buggy with Alice and you may ride my horse."

The young man acquiesced and mounted the horse. Allard rode next to Alice, but there was hardly a word passed between them. Alice was seething, but there was not much she could do. When they finally returned to the mansion, Allard stood on the veranda while she and the man said their goodbyes. He did, however, miss the young man silently handing Alice a small diamond ring. Her beautiful smile was the only answer he needed to his unasked question.

Despite her anger at Allard's tackiness, Alice was ecstatic. She was engaged to be married to the man she loved! Somehow, she'd convince her family. When they finally got to know him, they'd love him too. She just knew it.

She was so happy, that it didn't occur to her that she should hide the ring. That evening at dinner, her mother noticed the sparkle on her finger. Grabbing her daughter's hand, she looked aghast.

"What is that on your finger, Alice? My word, it looks like an engagement ring. The diamond is so small, though!"

Allard glanced at the ring.

"What are you thinking? There is no way you are going to marry that man!" he roared. "Give me that ring, so I can return it to him."

"No!"

"Yes! You will return it to him. Now take it off."

Seeing she would get nowhere, Alice removed the ring and put it in her pocket.

"Now, you will return the ring to him, do you hear me? And I don't want to hear any more about this man. Mother and I have discussed it, and we've decided that you will return to Charleston to finish your schooling. I've booked your passage. You'll be leaving in two days."

Tears of anger and frustration rolled down her cheeks. "You can't do this, Allard. I love him. We're going to be married."

"No, you're not. You will do as I say. I know you think me harsh, but truly it is for the best."

Days later, Alice found herself amid the hustle and bustle of Charleston. Alone, depressed, and still angry, she kept to herself, ignoring overtures of friendship from her new classmates. Some elements of Charleston did not suit her: the city was loud and busy, and sometimes less than refined. When not in class, she stayed in her small room, barely eating and grieving over her lost love. Her hand kept straying to the ribbon around her neck, a pink satin ribbon that held the diamond engagement ring, which she had not returned. She always wore it there, close to her heart.

Days passed into weeks, and weeks into months, and still Alice pined. She lost weight, and though she'd become even more beautiful, she looked pale and fragile, like some ethereal being not of this world.

It was in this frail state that she suddenly became ill. Chills and fever wracked her thin body, and by the time Allard, notified by the school's doctor, reached her side, she was delirious from malarial fever. She hardly had the ability to even acknowledge his presence. He quickly had her belongings packed and they began their trek back to the Hermitage.

The journey was long and arduous, with seven rivers to cross by ferry. It had rained the whole way, and the roadways on Murrell's Inlet were sandy and slippery. Several times, Allard had to get out of the carriage and help push it back onto the roadway. All the while, Alice fretted in the back of the carriage, semi-conscious from a burning fever. By the time they reached the Hermitage, she was much worse.

As Allard was lifting her from the carriage, the pink ribbon became uncovered and he saw the ring dangling there. Furious, he grabbed it from around her neck and threw it into the sea, raising a weak cry from Alice.

"My ring! Give me back my ring." But it was gone, disappeared beneath the gray water.

That night, Alice's body, wracked by pain and illness, and her spirit, diminished by her lost love, gave up the fight. Several days later, she was buried, wearing her favorite white ball gown, in the family plot at All Saints Cemetery near Pawleys Island. A plain marble slab was placed at the head of her grave—a marker with just one word—ALICE. Modern day visitors to her grave have worn a path around it, many believing that by circling it backwards thirteen times, they can summon her. When she is sighted, she always seems to be searching for something, one hand clutched protectively to her chest.

According to legend, she's spending eternity

searching for her lost ring and, it's said, she doesn't mind taking whatever is close. One young lady visiting Alice's gravesite reported that the ring on her finger suddenly flew off. It was a ring that, because of a weight gain, she'd been unable to remove for more than a year.

The spirit of Alice Flagg still wanders the halls of the Hermitage, which is a private residence. She's been seen entering the front door and silently ascending the staircase to her old bedroom on the second floor. Usually, she's seen in the evening or late night.

The Headless Soldier of Wedgefield Plantation

The Headless Soldier of Wedgefield Plantation

Georgetown is the birthplace of the American Revolution's greatest guerilla fighter. General Francis Marion, once a peaceful farmer, began his fighting career when the Cherokee began massacring settlers. A quick study, he learned their techniques for sneak attack and for disappearing into the swamps and forests for cover, a tactic that earned him the moniker "The Swamp Fox."

By the time the British sent a fleet of fifty ships to capture Charleston in 1776, Marion was already a brilliant and well-known strategist. Attacking from the unfinished fort on Sullivan's Island, he and his troops were able to cripple the entire British fleet, despite a lack of adequate ammunition. Marion's tactics saved Charleston and scored the first significant victory of the American Revolution.

Marion served as the colonel of the second South Carolina regiment until 1780, when Charleston fell and the regiment was surrendered to the British, along with five thousand other troops. Escaping capture,

Marion rounded up a band of rag tag soldiers and put together a troop that became known as Marion's Brigade.

The brigade consisted of 150 tattered patriots, whose only pay was the opportunity to fight for freedom from tyranny. Receiving neither food nor ammunition from the Continentals, they nevertheless staged a series of hit and run attacks that kept the war alive in South Carolina against overwhelming odds. They fought courageously until the arrival of General Nathan Greene and the American army, which helped to defeat the main British army under the command of General Cornwallis.

Although Marion was awarded a Congressional citation for wisdom and bravery, he and his men, deemed too ragged, were not invited to join the celebration when Charleston was finally wrested from British control. They did, however, win a place of honor in the history of the American Revolution.

Marion and his merry band used Georgetown as a base of operations during the year they were staging their raids on the British, and that town's Wedgefield Plantation played an important role in assisting them.

Wedgefield's history dates back to South Carolina's colonial period when Georgetown was first settled. Records show that it was a prospering plantation by 1750.

In the 1760s, the plantation changed owners and a second, two-story rectangular manor house was built. The first smaller house was used as a residence by the plantation overseer. The new owner was a prominent and wealthy man who owned Wedgefield in Georgetown, and a large home in Charleston, where he spent most of his time engaged in business and politics. Although not an office holder, he was influential on the political scene of the period.

When the American Revolution began, the owner of Wedgefield refused to take sides, despite the fact that his family was staunchly on the side of the Continentals. The owner's business was heavily supported by British interests, and he did not want to cut his own throat. Months passed and the owner began to find it difficult to remain neutral. At times, he found himself aiding the British; at others, he would help out the Americans.

When British forces took over Georgetown, making it a significant stronghold, he found it impossible to continue straddling the fence. He jumped down on the side of the Tories, raising the ire of his American-sympathizing family.

His daughter was living with him at the time, and, although she was a staunch American, she dared not speak out for fear of offending him and losing her home. She did find a way to lend her support, however, by approaching General Francis Marion and offering to become a spy for the cause. Her father's prominence gave her access to much information and, by keeping her eyes and ear open, she became one of Marion's most valuable secret agents. The information she passed on—using an alcove of the nearby Prince George Church as a secret place to pass on written information—greatly assisted in Marion's success in his attacks on British troops.

The British occupation of Georgetown filled the small town to capacity, necessitating the takeover of many plantations to house the British and Tory troops. Many of the larger homes were used as hospitals and some were used as prisons. This became the fate of Wedgefield. The manor was used as a hospital and the smaller house was used to house important American prisoners.

One of the most important prisoners kept here was the senile father of one of Marion's Brigade. The father, an arrogant and boastful man, had been present when many of the brigade's plans were being made, and it was feared that in his confusion, he might reveal damaging information. Marion desperately wanted him rescued.

Turning to his most trusted spy, Marion asked the daughter of Wedgefield's owner to be sure the old man was indeed interned there and to assist in his escape. The daughter, who was staying with her father at the family home in Charleston, sent word that she had seen the old man, his daughter, a niece, and his wife. They had been kept in the servant's quarters of the Charleston home for a night, where no one was allowed to speak to them. The next day they had all be taken away, though the young woman did not know for sure where. It wasn't too far, though, for the escort detail had returned in a timely manner. It was possible, she said, that they had been taken to Wedgefield, especially considering that her father had sent a small wagon of household goods to the plantation along with the escort detail.

In order to ascertain the true whereabouts of the prisoners, the woman asked her father to secure a

British detail to escort her to their Wedgefield Plantation, saying she needed to select poultry for their needs there in town, to talk to the carpenter to build some crates, and to remind him of the repairs that were needed in the town home.

Upon arrival at Wedgefield, she went into the house on the pretense of taking cookies to the injured soldiers. The first people she saw were the old man and his wife. As soon as possible, she reported the news to Marion's scout, and the two quickly devised an escape plan. Since she was thought of as loyal to the British, it was decided that she would plan a party for the soldiers to be held at the nearby Mansfield Plantation. All the soldiers guarding Wedgefield would be invited, a ploy that was sure to deplete the security of the makeshift prison.

Their plan worked almost perfectly. All the soldiers, save one poor soul, were allowed to attend the ball. After the party was in full swing, the young spy slipped away into the night, joining Marion's men as they galloped toward Wedgefield. The lone soldier left to guard the prisoners heard the horses coming, but believed them to be his comrades returning from the party.

He ran out to the road to greet them, probably

looking to see if they'd thought to bring him food and drink. The horsemen were almost upon him before he realized that it was not his buddies who were returning, but a cadre of Continentals, coming, no doubt, to free his prisoners.

Drawing his gun, he took aim at the closest horseman, who drew his weapon as well. Musket shots rang out simultaneously, but both bullets missed their mark. Still galloping full ahead, the horseman threw away his useless pistol and drew his saber. As he neared, he took a long sweep and instantly severed the guard's head from his body.

It was a gruesome sight, reported Marion's men. With blood spurting from his neck, the guard's body reeled about, tottering across the lawn before collapsing into a bloody, twitching heap. The head rolled across the roadway and disappeared into a ditch.

Unable to locate the head, the Americans retrieved the British soldier's body and buried it in the garden behind Wedgefield. They then freed the prisoners and transported them to Marion's camp. Mission accomplished.

For centuries now, there have been reports that the spirit of the British soldier is haunting the grounds of

Wedgefield. According to legend, strange sounds are heard before the spirit appears. Sometimes it's the sound of a distant roar and the clatter of horses' hooves on the roadway, usually occurring just before nightfall. The horrific manifestation of the British soldier then appears. His headless torso reels around the lawn, pistol in hand, in an obvious search for his missing head. If the sound of thundering hooves is not heard, his appearance may be heralded by the sound of dragging chains. The grisly sight appears only briefly before vanishing.

There have also been reports of sightings that occur late at night. When the phantom soldier appears at this time, usually on bright, moonlit nights, he is seen pacing up and down the porch at Wedgefield, as if he's still carrying out his duty guarding the important prisoners. On these occasions, it's said that his head is still attached to his body, and he does not provoke the same kind of fear experienced by the sight of his headless spirit.

The old manor house was razed in the 1930s and was replaced by the present mansion. Considered one of the Low Country's showplaces, it now serves as one of South Carolina's premier golf courses.

Since the renovation of the building, the headless soldier is not seen as often as before, but he does still haunt the section of the grounds where his body is supposedly buried. There also have been reports of strange, unexplainable noises inside the renovated manor. Many believe it to be the soldier, checking out his new digs.

A Most Spirited Inn

A Most Spirited Inn

Merridun, a stately antebellum mansion listed on the National Register of Historic Places, was built in 1855, by William Keenan, a wealthy local merchant and one-time mayor of the small town of Union. Known as the Keenan Plantation, the farm, at that time, consisted of four thousand acres of cultivated land.

The plantation was bought in 1876 by Union lawyer Benjamin Rice, who adjoined it to his existing plantation, creating a new eight thousand-acre farm, growing mainly cotton. Rice, who used the Union house as his main residence, completed a major renovation in the early 1880s.

It was around this same time that Thomas C. (T.C.) Duncan came to Union to work with his grandfather, Benjamin Rice. In 1885, he married and brought his new bride, Fannie Merriman, to live with him at the plantation that he, by now, had inherited from his grandparents. He renamed it "Merridun," combining the three surnames—Merriman, Rice, and Duncan.

T.C. was an influential man who, by 1893, had almost single-handedly restored the town of Union to the wealth and power it had enjoyed before the Civil War. Introducing the textile industry to Union, he built the town's first successful cotton mill within sight of his mansion. And that's not all. Both an industrial and political leader, he served two terms in the South Carolina House of Representatives, constructing the mill in Buffalo, Union's B.U.C. Railroad, and the hydro-electric plant.

After inheriting Merridun, T.C. completed an extensive remodel of the original manor, replacing the double piazza's plain Doric columns with Corinthian columns and adding side wing marble porticos.

Inside, the 7900-square foot mansion contained—and still does—a stunning curved stairway, large foyers on both floors, a music room, seven bedrooms, multiple bathrooms, and a third story cupola. The carriage barn still houses T.C.'s favorite carriage. Unique architectural features added include frescoed ceilings in the music room and dining room, stenciling, and beautiful chandeliers.

The Duncans experienced both happiness and tragedy here. Two sons died at a young age, but their three daughters lived long lives. Seven generations of the Benjamin Rice family lived at Merridun before it was sold in 1990.

Today the beautiful mansion is a luxury bed and breakfast inn. Nestled among shady oaks and magnolias, it's been lovingly restored to its former glory. Taking in the inn's more than one hundred-fifty-year history, visitors can easily envision saucy Southern belles sweeping down the magnificent curved stairway or strolling across the elegant marble verandas. They can sit and rock away the hours on those cool verandas, glass of ice tea and book in hand, or nap in one of the hammocks strung between the stately oaks.

They shouldn't be surprised if they're awakened by a ghostly touch, though. For the Inn at Merridun is quite a spirited place, and I'm not just talking about fun things to do. According to legend, as many as ten different ghosts frequent the inn. First, there's T.C. and Fannie, who seem to have never left. They're said to be connected to the pennies that seem to show up from nowhere, and often owners and guests will catch a whiff of T.C.'s favorite cigar or Fannie's old-fashioned perfume.

Another spirit wandering the halls may be that of

Mary Anne Wallace, a spinster sister of one of the 1870 owners—Benjamin Rice's wife maybe? Anyway, Mary Anne is a short, stout, and quite buxom lady. She's seen wearing a blue-gray dress.

There's the ghost of a little white dog that likes to jump in bed with friendly guests. If he doesn't like them, he has no compunction against growling at them.

One ghost enjoys playing the harpsichord and the piano, and may often wake guests with a serenade. Another ghost is a gadget freak. This spirit likes to fiddle with the household appliances, locking food in the digital oven while it's baking and fiddling with the computer keyboard.

The last two known spirits are those of Native Americans who predate the mansion. They have been seen outside and have been heard playing their drums.

The Gray Man of Pawleys Island

The Gray Man of Pawleys Island

Pawleys Island's Gray Man is a heck of a weather-man. For more than one hundred years, this ghost, one of South Carolina's most famous, has appeared to area residents to warn them of coming hurricanes. As the legend goes, he's appeared before every major hurricane to hit Pawleys Island. He warns the person to whom he has appeared that he should pack up his family and leave the island. If the person heeds the warning, it's said, his home is spared by the hurricane.

There's some disagreement about the true identity of this helpful spirit. There are three different stories surrounding the mystery. The first concerns an eager fiancé killed in a tragic accident.

This first story is one of star-crossed lovers, both from prominent families in Charleston. Seems there was a young couple who was very much in love. The woman was beautiful and had many suitors, none of whom seemed to interest her. She instead fell in love

130

with a wild and reckless young man, who also happened to be her cousin.

The families of the couple both objected to the relationship and did their best to end it. The young man's father sent him to school in Europe, hoping, I suppose, "out of sight, out of mind." Not long after arriving in France, word was sent that the young man had died in a duel. The girl was brokenhearted. She went into seclusion for many months, refusing all callers.

Ah, but life goes on. A year later, the family was visited by a wealthy widower, a rice planter from the Waccamaw area. The widower was instantly besotted with the still grief-stricken daughter. He wooed her patiently and gently, finally winning her affection, and asking her father for her hand in marriage.

The couple enjoyed a privileged life, wintering at the widower's large plantation on Waccamaw Neck and summering at his home on Pawleys Island. Things were going well until the Revolution broke out. The widower left to fight the British, serving as a captain under General Francis Marion.

During the summer of 1778, while the widower was still away fighting, his wife took the servants and moved into the summer home on Pawleys Island. They had been there only a few nights when a violent storm hit, causing a ship to founder just off the coast of the island. A survivor struggled from the water and was found by the servants. They brought him to the house to give him food and water, telling him that the master was away, but the mistress would give him shelter from the storm.

Told of the man's plight, the wife came downstairs to greet her new guest. When she walked into the kitchen and saw the man, she screamed and fainted. The man let out an anguished cry, bolted from the house, and disappeared into the storm.

Reviving their mistress, the servants learned that she believed she had seen a ghost, for the mysterious survivor sitting in her kitchen was her long lost love, killed in a duel years before. It was later learned that, while endeavoring to make it to Charleston, he had contracted yellow fever and died. It's he that haunts Pawleys Island. He's the famous Gray Man, who warns residents of coming storms.

The next Gray Man story is another tale of star-crossed lovers from Pawleys Island. The two were engaged, and the young man had been away on business for several months. Returning from his long sea voyage, he was so eager to see his beautiful fiancée, that he took a shortcut through the marshland.

He was riding at a full gallop, when his horse charged into a pool of quicksand. Though his trusted servant, who was riding behind him, tried to save him, it was no use. The man and his horse sank into the quicksand, never to be seen again.

The young fiancée was devastated by the loss of her true love. After his funeral, she took to walking the beach of Pawleys Island, crying and remembering the happy days she'd spent with him on this very beach. One day as she strolled through the sand, she looked down the beach to see a man in a gray suit. She blinked and squinted into the sunlight, trying to see more clearly, for surely her eyes were deceiving her. The man in the gray suit looked like her fiancé, just as she'd last seen him departing on his business trip.

She stopped and as the man neared, he spoke to her urgently. "You are in danger. You must leave the island at once!" He then disappeared.

The girl ran home and told her parents of her strange encounter. The family quickly packed up and left the island. That night one of the worst hurricanes ever hit the island, demolishing every house but theirs.

And then there's the one that claims the Gray Man is the spirit of Plowden Charles Jeannerette Weston, the owner of Hagley Plantation, now the Pelican Inn.

Plowden Weston was a favored son of an obscenely wealthy rice plantation baron in Georgetown. A privileged child, he was reared at Laurel Hill Plantation, where he was given any little thing his heart desired. His parents doted on him, and though his father was staunchly anti-British, he wanted his son to have a proper British education.

In his younger years, Plowden was privately educated by a British tutor. Then, at the age of twelve, his whole family temporarily moved to England so that he could be educated there. The family eventually returned to South Carolina, but Plowden stayed on in England to finish his education at Cambridge. It was there that he met and fell in love with Emily Frances Esdaile, the beautiful daughter of an English baronet.

Because of his father's animosity toward the British, Plowden feared his father would not approve of the union. His father, however, reluctantly gave his blessing, but kicked off a competition on which papa would be the most generous. When Emily's father gave the couple a dowry of seven thousand pounds, Plowden's dad endowed them with seventy thousand pounds, a house in London, a house in Geneva, and Hagley Plantation in Georgetown. The contest was over. Even an English baronet couldn't compete with that kind of wealth.

Plowden and Emily married in August 1847, and settled into Hagley Plantation, with its vast and fertile fields of rice extending from the cypress-lined Waccamaw River to the blue Atlantic. Like many Low Country planters, eager to escape the humid summer with its malaria-bearing mosquitoes, Plowden and Emily made plans to build a summer home on Pawleys Island. Not only would a summer home on the island help alleviate the intense heat, particularly important to the couple acclimated to the cooler weather of England, but it would also give them a vacation from the demands of Hagley Plantation.

They put Hagley's master carpenter, Renty Tucker, in charge of construction on the new house. Choosing a plot behind the protection of the dunes, the elevated foundation and lower floor were constructed of strong timber. Each piece of lumber used was hand-hewed and numbered at Hagley before it was transported by boat to Pawleys Island. Handmade arches and columns decorated the wide lower-level porch, while the upper level of the house rose above the trees and sheltering dunes. A second-floor piazza, accessible from the upstairs bedrooms, faced the Atlantic. Reports are that Emily and Plowden spent much time here, gazing out over the Atlantic and, no doubt, contemplating their good fortune.

In addition to the house, the couple built a huge chapel that could seat as many as two hundred slaves. One of thirteen slave chapels on Waccamaw Neck, it had stained-glass windows from England, hand-carved oak choir stalls, and a granite baptismal fountain.

Plowden and Emily spent a blissful decade together, dividing their time between Hagley and Pawleys Island. By the late 1850s, however, the growing dissension between the North and South began to splinter their peaceful existence. Plowden, a published historian and fiery orator, gave many speeches and published articles warning of the coming war. As a plantation and slave owner, he supported the Southern cause.

When the Civil War began, Plowden became the company commander of the Georgetown Rifle Guard, personally outfitting the 150 men in his charge. During the early part of the war, he and Emily frequently entertained the regiment and their ladies at his Pawleys Island home.

At one point, rumor was the island was to be attacked. The Rifle Guard was ordered to gather within a few miles of Hagley Plantation. The threat turned out to be a false alarm. A whole regiment, all dressed up and nowhere to go. Not to worry! Plowden invited the entire company over to Hagley for a sumptuous three-course dinner, each course served with a different vintage wine from the Hagley cellar.

All the fun ended when Plowden contracted tuberculosis near the end of the war. His friends in the state legislature, knowing he wouldn't give up his command without a good reason, engineered his election to lieutenant governor of South Carolina. He accepted the position, but was unable to serve for long, for the tuberculosis worsened, and by January 1864, he lay dying in Conway, South Carolina.

At Plowden's request, Hagley's servants were brought to Conway, where they each received a gift for their years of service. His last moments were spent with Emily. After his death, his body was transported by canoe down the Waccamaw River to Hagley. He was buried next to his father in the churchyard of the All Saints Waccamaw Episcopal Church, where he and Emily were married.

Because of Plowden Weston's devotion to his Pawleys Island home, many people believe he is the Gray Man. In life, he warned his friends and neighbors of the perils of a coming war. In death, he warns of the dangers of impending storms.

There's one more version of the Gray Man story. And this one includes a Gray Lady, Plowden, and Emily's old Pawleys Island home.

After Plowden and Emily's deaths, the house was inherited by Plowden's cousins, Mr. and Mrs. William St. Julian Mazyck, who operated the home as a bed and breakfast. It was next owned by the Weavers, and is now owned and run as the Pelican Inn by the Evans family.

When the home was owned by the Weavers, there were numerous supernatural occurrences. The first happened to Mrs. Weaver when she and her cook were in the kitchen making homemade bread. Absorbed in her work, Weaver turned to find a woman standing behind her, hands on hips and eyes steadfastly fixed on the bread-making process. She was wearing a long dress of gray gingham with tiny pearl buttons running down the bodice, and a white apron, said Weaver. The woman's features appeared to be French, and according to Weaver, she wore a disapproving expression. She seemed to be saying, "You'd better get it right."

Weaver said although the woman's features were clear, it was obvious that she was not of this world. As Weaver watched, she just faded away. The woman in gray gingham became a familiar sight at the Pelican Inn. Many guests saw her and would not realize on a first sighting that she was a ghost. She was most often seen walking up the stairway toward the bedrooms and when guests learned of these frequent appearances, they would sit on the sitting room sofa and wait for her to appear.

The Gray Man also appeared to Weaver. He wore nineteenth century clothing and, like the Gray Woman, he became a regular feature of the inn. It seems he liked to cause a bit of mischief every now and then. Weaver's daughter sometimes related the story about her sister-in-law, Gayle, who was helping around the inn. She was upstairs cleaning the bedrooms when a stack of magazines caught her attention. Fancying a break, she picked up one of the publications and began to page through it, nonchalantly leaning against a table.

She'd been reading for several minutes, when she felt a tug at her shirt tail. Thinking it was one of the family having her on, she ignored the tug and kept reading. Again, came the tug on her shirt tail. Suddenly, it occurred to her that, because of the inn's hardwood floors, it would be impossible for someone to sneak up on her—someone of flesh and bone, anyway. She started and looked around. Sure enough, there was no one there. Figuring that the Gray Man didn't like that she was goofing off when she should be busy, she immediately went back to work.

Many thought the Gray Woman and the Gray Man to be the apparitions of Plowden and Emily Weston. They'd be wrong, however. Weaver said when being interviewed about the ghosts by a local paper, she was shown an assortment of nineteenth-century photographs. She instantly recognized the two apparitions as Mr. and Mrs. William St. Julian Mazyck, cousins of Plowden. Emily and Plowden had no children and so when they died, the house went to the Mazycks, who operated it as a bed and breakfast for many years. Weaver said she knew the Mazycks had loved the inn and she believes it's their spirits who are haunting it.

About the Author

Lynne L. Hall is a native Southerner who is well acquainted with the people and places that make these stories so interesting to read and share. Her work has appeared in *Cosmopolitan*, *Penthouse*, *Popular Science*, *Physical*, and in many other magazines. She is the author of the Strange But True series of books that includes volumes on Alabama, Florida, Georgia, Virginia, and Tennessee.

Other ghostly tales from Lynne's pen are found in *Tennessee Ghosts*, *North Carolina Ghosts*, and *Florida Ghosts*.